Alef-Bet Yoga
for Kids

Kar-Ben Publishing
A division of Lerner Publishing Group, Inc.
241 First Avenue North
Minneapolis, MN 55401 U.S.A.
1-800-4KARBEN

www.karben.com

Library of Congress Cataloging-in-Publication Data

Goldeen, Bill.
    Alef bet yoga for kids / by Bill Goldeen and Ruth Goldeen.
       p.   cm.
    ISBN 978–0–8225–8756–9 (lib. bdg. : alk. paper)
    1. Hebrew language—Alphabet—Juvenile literature. I. Goldeen, Ruth. II. Title.
  PJ4589.G585 2009
  492.4'813—dc22   2007048360

Manufactured in the United States of America
1 2 3 4 5 6 – PA – 14 13 12 11 10 09

Introducing Alef-Bet Yoga: "Being" the Hebrew alphabet!

Children are natural yogis! The process of "being" an object or animal is very appealing to a child. In *Alef-Bet Yoga for Kids*, children have an opportunity to learn the Hebrew alphabet in a very experiential way by actually becoming the letters.

In this book, traditional and modified yoga poses are used to create all the Hebrew letters. While joyfully learning the Alef-Bet, children gain the benefits from the stretching, strengthening, balance, body awareness and focus offered by each pose.

Once the Alef-Bet poses have been learned, children can enjoy "playing" with the letters. The poses can be combined to spell a child's Hebrew name or act out Alef-Bet songs!

Alef א

Bet ב

Gimmel ג

Daled ד

Hey ה

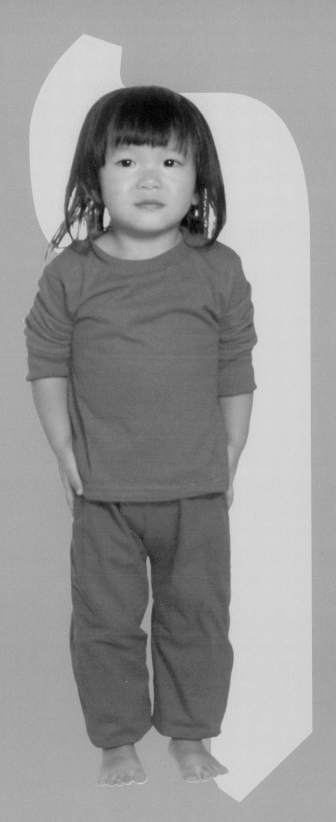

Vav ו

Zayin ז

Chet ח

Tet ט

Yod '

Chaf כ

Lamed ל

Mem מ

Nun נ

Samech ס

Pey פ

Tzadi צ

Kuf ק

Resh ר

Shin ש

Taf ת

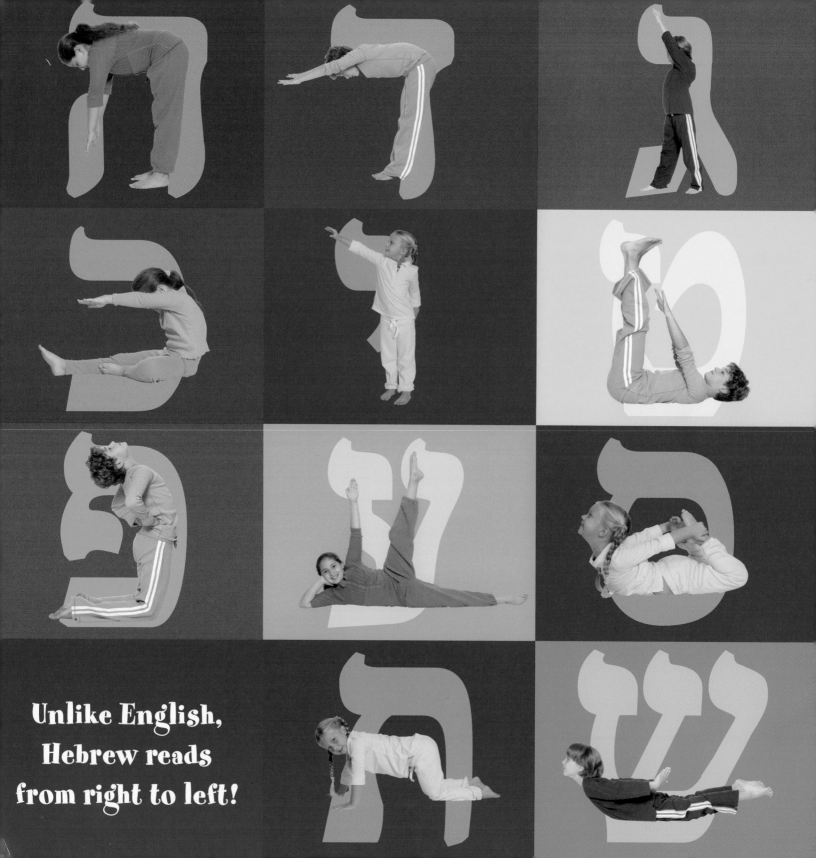

Unlike English,
Hebrew reads
from right to left!

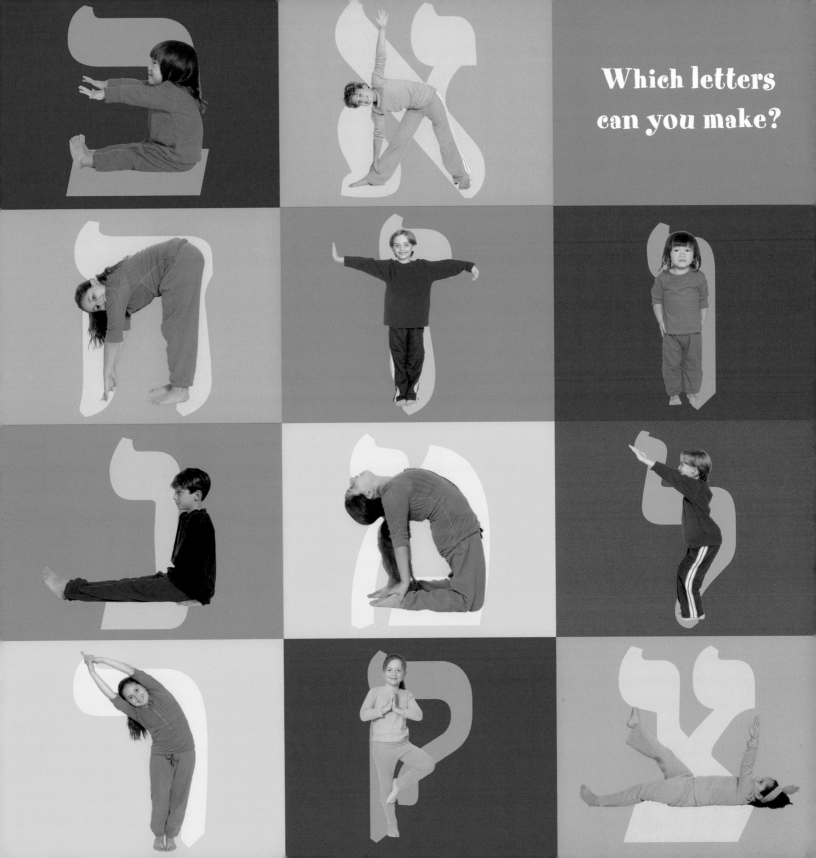

Which letters
can you make?

Glossary of Alef-Bet Yoga Poses

Alef pose is the traditional Triangle Pose, or *Trikonasana*. This pose involves extension of trunk and all four limbs of the body. The pose challenges our strength, flexibility and balance. Children can be told to use their bodies to touch the earth while reaching for the sky!

Bet is a variation of *Dandasana*, or Extended Stick or Staff Pose. This pose involves straight back, legs and arms and working on good upright sitting posture.

Gimmel is a variation of *Virabhadrasana I*, or Warrior I Pose. Children should be told to reach toward the sky, filling their bodies with strength.

Daled is a variation of *Uttanasana* or Forward Extension Pose. Children work on finding their flat back, while in a standing position. In this pose the child can reach toward the future.

Hey is a variation of *Prasarita Padottanasana*, or Extended Foot/Leg Pose. This pose teaches children to strengthen, lengthen and relax at the same time.

Vav is *Tadasana*, or Mountain Pose. This pose helps children to strengthen and straighten the back, improving posture, while making the mind alert.

Zayin is a variation of *Tadasana*, or Mountain Pose. It adds strengthening benefits for arms and shoulders to the postural benefits of the pose.

Chet is a variation of *Uttanasana*, or Intensely Stretch Pose. This pose helps to strengthen the organs, while improving concentration.

Tet is *Navasana*, or Boat Pose. This pose helps children strengthen the muscles of the stomach and back.

Yod is represented by the hand. The child stabilizes the trunk, shoulder and arm, while concentrating on a specific shape of the hand.

Chaf is a variation of the *Janu Sirsansana*, or Knee-Head Pose. This pose strengthens a child's postural muscles and stretches hamstrings, while toning internal organs.

Lamed is *Utkatasana*, or High/Mighty/Superior Pose. In this pose the child squeezes legs together while crouching to sit on a "make-believe chair" and reaching for the sky. This pose strengthens ankles, calves, inner thighs and back.

Mem is *Ushtrasana*, or Camel Pose. While reaching for feet the child's chest reaches for the sky and head relaxes backwards. This pose helps remove stiffness in the neck and shoulders, helps the child develop trust and is fun!

Nun is *Dandasana*, or Staff/Rod Pose. This pose encourages a child's good sitting posture.

Samech is *Dhanurasana*, or Bow Pose. This challenging pose improves a child's spinal flexibility while expanding chest and lungs.

Ayin is modified from *Anantasana*, or Endless/Infinite Pose. This pose strengthens a child's back while stretching the hamstrings. The child reaches both legs and the up-stretched arm "endlessly."

Pey is a beginning pose working towards *Ushtrasana* (Camel or Mem) and *Kapotasana* or Pigeon Pose. This pose helps make the child's spine strong and flexible, opens the throat and chest and helps develop a sense of courage.

Tzadi is modified from *Urdhva Prasarita Padasana*, or Upwards Stretched Foot Pose. This pose helps to trim and strengthen the child's waist, massages internal abdomenal organs and aids circulation.

Kuf is a variation of *Vrkshasana* or Tree Pose. This pose helps the child find postural stability for balance and improves concentration. The child should imagine being deeply rooted, while growing tall.

Resh is *Ardha Chandrasana* or Half Moon Pose. This pose offers a child lateral stretch, opens the rib cage, and deepens breathing.

Shin is modified from *Shalabhasana* or Grasshopper/Locust Pose. We turn this into Shark Pose by clasping hands behind the back, to represent the fin. This pose strengthens a child's back muscles while increasing shoulder flexibility.

Tav is a variation of the *Marjarasana*, or cat pose. The full pose offers a wonderful spinal massage, alternately arching the back upwards (with an exhalation) and arching the back down with the head and tail up (during the inhalation). Make sure children don't forget to "meow"!

This book project has allowed Bill Goldeen to blend his passions for portrait photography, Jewish education and yoga. Bill is a professional photographer with degrees in vocal music performance and history. He studied Holocaust education at Yad Vashem in Jerusalem and is a docent at the Virginia Holocaust Museum in Richmond, VA. Bill is also a classical chamber singer with the Charlottesville early music group, Zephyrus.

Ruth Goldeen combines her appreciation of yoga and her passion for working with children. She is a pediatric occupational therapist at Kluge Children's Rehabilitation Center at the University of Virginia. She has a Master's Degree in Early Childhood Education, with a Special Needs emphasis. Ruth teaches kids' yoga, including classes for children with special needs.

Bill and Ruth live with their two children and pets, in Charlottesville, VA.